A GENERATION OF INDUSTRIAL PEACE

Mass interview with a group of Jersey Standard employees is conducted by Elmo Roper. The written interview, by avoiding embarrassment to individuals, elicits honest responses.

STUART CHASE

A Generation of Industrial Peace

Thirty Years of Labor Relations at Standard Oil Company (N.J.)

STANDARD OIL COMPANY (N. J.)

1947

HD 6961
C 48

CONTENTS

PREFACE

FOR some thirty years now, men and management of companies affiliated with Standard Oil Company (New Jersey) have worked together in harmony and understanding based on a philosophy of mutual respect. This record has been a matter of understandable pride to the Jersey organization.

Because tranquillity by its very nature is unspectacular and unnewsworthy, people in general have been little aware of the steady march of the years of peace.

The Jersey Company believes that this story is one well worth the telling. Therefore Stuart Chase, writer on economics and related subjects who has an abiding interest in the impact of science and machinery on human beings, was invited to survey Jersey's labor relations and report his findings in THE LAMP.

Mr. Chase was assured complete freedom to reach his own conclusions, whether favorable or unfavorable to the company.

He spent several months on the assignment. He visited refineries at Bayonne and Baton Rouge. He chatted with stillmen, with union leaders and representatives of management.

The article which appears on the following pages is the result. Written in Mr. Chase's remarkably lucid and entertaining style, it is the story primarily of a philosophy, rather than a mechanism, which has enabled men to work with men—in peace for a generation.

Veteran employee Daniel V. Heeney, a boiler shop worker, has been with Jersey Standard more than forty years. His is not an exceptional case in a company whose employee turnover rate has not, even in wartime, exceeded 22 per cent in the past fifteen years.

Union and management sit down together at Bayonne. Clement A. Hurley, president of Standard Refinery Union, Inc., addresses a grievance meeting requested by the union. Such meetings are in addition to regularly scheduled bimonthly joint conferences.

PART ONE

The Historical Record

ON A SUMMER DAY in 1915 there was a pitched battle in the streets of Bayonne, New Jersey. Strikers from the Standard Oil refinery were throwing bricks and stones, the police were firing their revolvers. When the smoke cleared away, at least one striker lay dead, and many on both sides were wounded.

The still-cleaners and other laborers at the refinery had sent representatives to management some days before, asking for better working conditions and higher wages. The general superintendent refused to see them. They tried again; and again he refused. On the night of July 20 they voted to strike.

Next morning the incoming shift found a line of pickets around the entrance to the plant. Many joined the strikers, the rest went home. The refinery gates were locked. Rioting began in the streets. Fires were set; tank cars of oil, box cars of merchandise, a company pump house went up in flames. Guards were hastily armed and sworn in, but the situation was out of control. Only when the Bayonne Chamber of Commerce telegraphed the Governor for troops did the battle in the streets end.

The strikers, who numbered 1,500, complained that foremen mistreated them. They were continually cursed out, they said. To settle grudges, foremen were detaining cleaners in the hot stills, with temperatures up to 250° F. The strikers

9

demanded a fifty-hour week, time and a half for overtime, a 15 per cent increase in wages, and no discrimination because of strike activity. An agent from the IWW[1] tried to get the strikers to join his union, but the men said they wanted their own local organization, and threw him out of the meeting. This is important in view of later history.

With the help of mediators the trouble subsided temporarily. But the next year it broke out again with great violence in the paraffin works at the Bayonne refinery. The police were hastily summoned as before. There was another fight, some say worse than the first, and more men went to the hospital and the cemetery.

The strikes at Bayonne, shortly before America entered World War I, were a bloody, bitter business. One of the demands of the workers read: "We request humane treatment at the hands of the foremen and superiors in place of the brutal kicking and punching we now receive without provocation." Whether true or not, this charge illustrates how the men *felt* about their superiors. Worker and management made a bad team in 1916. In this, Jersey Standard[2] was no different from most big corporations during those years of barricades, IWW agitation, armed guards and sudden death.

Since that time in October 1916, however, about thirty years ago, there has been no violence, and only a few local work stoppages in Jersey Standard. The most extensive of the latter was the strike of about 1,000 seamen operating tankers

[1] The Industrial Workers of the World was organized in 1905. It was "a revolutionary industrial union," the purpose of which was "to organize the working class industrially not only for everyday struggles against employers but for the final overthrow of capitalism." (*Encyclopedia of the Social Sciences.*)

[2] The terms "Jersey Standard" or "Standard" as used in the following pages refer to operating affiliates of Standard Oil Company (New Jersey).

in 1939, which lasted two months. The big strike in the oil industry in the fall of 1945, with 60,000 out, passed almost completely over Jersey Standard. One small plant of the Humble Oil & Refining Company at Corpus Christi, Texas, however, was closed down for three days.

Back to the old shop. Why?

An Army poll asked GI's in World War II if they planned to go back to the old job when they left the service. Fifty per cent said they did not want to go back; they wanted something different.

But of the 7,321 Jersey Standard employees who were released from the Army or Navy up to April 1946, 6,840 headed for the old job and got it. Often they got a better one, as we shall see later. That works out to 93.4 per cent actually returning, against the general Army figure of 50 per cent desiring to return.[3]

What is the reason for this drastic break with normal statistics? What kind of magnet has the company got?

Turnover rate among employees in many companies runs up to 100 per cent or more per year.[4] The Hoover study on waste in industry, published in 1921, reported the average rate in the metal trades at 160 per cent, with one plant hitting 360 per cent. The turnover rate at Jersey Standard, however, has never exceeded 22 per cent in the last fifteen years of war and depression, with a low of 8 per cent in 1937. In the Bayonne refinery in 1944, it was 4 per cent. The last figure sounds

[3] The American Telephone and Telegraph Company says that more than 90 per cent of its men have come back.

[4] A turnover rate of 100 per cent means that if there were ten men in the plant at the beginning of the year, ten men were hired and ten went out during the year, to keep the force constant.

less incredible when we discover that three out of every four men at Bayonne have been with the company *twenty years or more*. One would expect the place to look like an old men's home, but it doesn't, though the tempo is rather more sedate at Bayonne than elsewhere.

All the above figures indicate that men like to work for Jersey Standard better than they like to work for American companies generally. Again why?

Where it all began

In trying to find an unprejudiced answer to these questions, we must follow the story back at least as far as the famous "Ludlow Massacre," shortly before the violent troubles at Bayonne.

A strike had been called by the United Mine Workers against the Colorado Fuel and Iron Company. Following the usual pattern of the times, strikers and their families were promptly evicted from company houses. They pitched tents on adjacent land. One group of tents was called the "Ludlow Camp." On April 20, 1914, state militia fired into this tent colony, killing not only strikers but their wives and children. Twenty-one died.

Throughout the nation people were horrified at the tragedy, among them John D. Rockefeller, Jr., whose family owned a large block of stock in the Colorado Fuel and Iron Company. He resolved that this kind of thing must never happen again in any company in which he had an interest. He called into consultation Mackenzie King[5] and Clarence J. Hicks, a specialist in labor relations then employed by the International

[5] Mr. King, now Prime Minister of Canada, was at that time employed by the Rockefeller Foundation as an industrial relations adviser.

12

Harvester Company. All three went to Colorado for a personal investigation of the massacre. In due course, Mr. Hicks and Mr. King worked out a plan for employee representation, along the line of the Whitley Shop Councils which were winning favor in Britain, and offered it to the mine workers for their approval.

At first the miners would have none of it. But when they found it was given in good faith, with no bias because of union membership, they accepted it. They elected representatives to confer with the company and set up grievance machinery. The first joint conference was held at Pueblo, Colorado, October 2, 1915, with Messrs. Rockefeller, King and Hicks in attendance. The management-labor situation in the mines began to improve. The company built new houses, camps, hospitals, schools. Mr. Hicks stayed on to administer the program.

After the Bayonne strikes, A. C. Bedford, then president of Jersey Standard, decided to see what the Colorado plan could accomplish in New Jersey. His situation, as the diplomats say, was deteriorating rapidly. A war was going on, though this country had not yet entered it. There was already a heavy demand for oil, and a heavier one in prospect. Production was needed—not strikes. So Mr. Hicks was invited to come East and introduce the employee representation plan in Jersey Standard.

When Mr. Hicks came to Jersey Standard, there was no established institution which could enroll his workers and protect them from the traditional autocratic type of management. True, there were two nation-wide labor organizations at the time, but neither could be of use in this particular case. The workers in New Jersey would have nothing to do with the IWW, and threw an organizer out of their meeting, as we have seen. The AF of L, on the other hand, was not structurally competent to handle oil workers, or indeed any of the new mass production industries. It was a federation of craft unions. A refinery, steel mill, rubber factory, chemical plant, organized by crafts would make no sense. Most mass production workers at that time were semi-skilled machine tenders or watchers. Furthermore, Mr. Hicks wanted to get Negroes, women and laboratory workers into his plan, and the AF of L in 1918 had few places for them.

So Mr. Hicks and his colleagues had to devise a self-contained institution which would give workers a strong union to fall back upon, for there was *no such outside union in sight*. He set up a local union, but it was only one stone in his wall; one means to a larger end. The end was an attempt to build a team in which workers would be satisfied.

The good old days

Before telling what Mr. Hicks did and how it came out, suppose we look briefly at an oil refinery of thirty years ago. It was not the streamlined more or less automatically controlled structure of today.

Out in New Jersey a veteran foreman described the good old days to me. The only recreation, he said, was the corner saloon. None of your la-dee-da softball teams or bowling contests. The peak of this recreation, he said, was called a "boilermaker and his helper," a potent slug of straight rye with a beer chaser. When foremen wanted more men they went out to the gate and picked them by intuition. "Now they measure 'em, blood test 'em, run 'em through a rat maze; phooey!" said my friend. "Still, we get more people who talk American."

14

"Talk American?" I asked.

"Mostly all foreigners in those days. Firemen on the stills got seventeen cents an hour. Now they get $1.45. The stillman and his helper were on duty for twenty-four hours when the shift changed once a week. It was a hell of a job trying to keep awake; you got fired if you went to sleep. Yes, the men are more educated now; they talk so you can understand them; they live better, have cars, go off on a two or three weeks' vacation every year. But they're not the gorillas they used to be. No sir, they can't take it like they could." My friend heaved a sigh. "Maybe it's all for the best."

Refining petroleum at first was hardly more exact than making bathtub gin. You dumped crude oil into a vat, or still, and built a fire under it. The first vapor to come off was probably gasoline, and you threw it away as a waste product. Next came kerosene, which was the payoff. Then the lighter lubricating oils, then the heavy oils. You scraped the muck out of the still and started another batch.

The tower still came in around 1909. It was somewhat more efficient, but not much.

Pressure stills

With automobiles came a roaring demand for gasoline. The pressure still was introduced after 1912 to meet the demand —a steel shell about thirty feet long, in which a couple of hundred barrels of oil were heated to 700° F. under seventy-five pounds of pressure. When it blew up—as one did now and then—a lot of men stopped work forever.

The best description I know of these pressure stills was written by Edward J. Nichols in a novel about the oil industry called *Danger: Keep Out*. Everyone interested in oil should

15

read it; meanwhile I will quote a few lines. It was based on a refinery in the Chicago area.

> If you fired on the new pressures, you had six stills, and there was a potential nervous breakdown in each one. Use your bar on Number 1; keep it out of Number 3; throw more coal on Number 2; keep your eye on the peepholes; you got a hot bottom on Number 3; 5 and 6 are dropping off a half-point; Number 4 is boosting; watch for a change in the wind that will knock you off balance on every still. Above all, keep your eye on that bottom in Number 3! . . . Otherwise, there's nothing to it except throwing in your 15 to 20 tons of coal for 10 hours on day shift, more coal in the 14-hour night shift . . . Almost anything could happen on the pressures, and about everything did.

A pressure still operated for forty-eight hours; then it had to be cleaned out for the next run of product. When the temperature dropped to about 250° F., a workman crawled inside, padded like an Eskimo, and with a big iron bar began to chip and scrape the tarry residue left on the bottom. A few hours later it would have been cool enough for anyone to do the job, but empty stills do not make money. Also the tar came off more easily when stills were hot. So these men—mostly foreigners, at six dollars for less than half a day's work—speeded it up. "Mike could hardly write his name in English, but plenty of white collars around the plant didn't touch his pay check. Of course he had it coming; the gases and the heat would probably get him in the end." You remember that this infernal task of still cleaning was connected with one of the principal grievances of the Bayonne strikers in 1915.

All this has gone. Trial-and-error has given way to scientific measurement. The old cylindrical stills, with their "lookboxes," have all but disappeared before the pipe stills and

Hiring men in "the good old days" was a hit-or-miss operation. The job hunters queued up at the gate, and the superintendent picked as many likely looking candidates as he needed.

Personnel specialists now interview prospective employees of Jersey Standard. The careful selection of men for jobs has helped to reduce the company's employee turnover rate.

RESEARCH CHEMIST

cracking towers, where no man sees the oil, fires the oil. It is all done by remote control, by throwing switches and watching dials, by instruments which never sleep. The scientists did not take over, however, without a battle, as Mr. Nichols makes plain.

> Gus couldn't take the chemists. Too much fussing around, nosing in this and that, asking about everything, taking notes, bringing trick meters out from the lab and pinning them up all over the place. They had bees up their pants. What was the idea? . . . If you fired stills a certain way in 1903, you fired them the same way in 1921 . . . Nobody would ever learn a job if chemists and engineers were going to be popping out of every coal bunker with some new harebrained notion . . . They said that once a chemist was caught around the stills and thrown in. Yes, they threw the chemist in, and an old stillman, looking at the product coming off, said, "By God, he lowered the gravity fifteen points!"

Representation: 1918-1923

Ahead of the high-powered chemists, however, came Clarence J. Hicks, who had assisted in the organization of Colorado Fuel and Iron. His first step in New Jersey was to invite workers by secret ballot to elect representatives who would then confer with the management. His offer was accepted.

The initial election was held at the Bayonne plant on March 27, 1918, during both day and night shifts. The timekeeper handed every wage earner a ballot, on which he wrote the name of the fellow worker he wanted to represent him. More than 90 per cent of the workers voted, in fourteen departments, including boilermakers and blacksmiths, carpenters and machinists, pipefitters and tinsmiths, yard labor, watchmen, still cleaners, stillmen, barrel factory workers, and so on. Thirty-seven representatives were chosen at Bayonne—one for every 150 men.

During the first fifteen months, thirty-four joint conferences were held at Bayonne between the workers' representatives and management, covering such matters as wage rates, working conditions, promotion and discharge grievances, hours, sanitation, housing conditions. Machinery for handling grievances was immediately set up, but real collective bargaining for wages and hours came somewhat later.

Workers were encouraged to settle personal grievances with foremen on the spot, before the rancor spread. As a mechanic said to me in New Jersey: "Grievances are like snowballs. They start small, but, boy, they grow! You've got to stop 'em early."

If the worker and his foreman could not settle a problem, then the worker's representative was called in. If the three of them could not settle it, then the worker could appeal right up the management ladder to the president of the company. With this flexible machinery behind him, the worker was no longer afraid to talk it out with his foreman. Tension began to relax in the New Jersey plants.

At the outset, both workers and management were pretty skeptical. "A lotta hooey," said many of the former. "They'll try and run the place," said some of the latter.

But after a year's trial, one of the workers' representatives got up in a joint conference and observed: "We were doubting Thomases, we delegates, a year ago, but since then the scales of suspicion have fallen from our eyes . . . The men are now confident of a square deal."

18

Why did the scales fall? Because managers had followed Mr. Hicks' philosophy and had really begun to trust the workers. When people trust you, you almost automatically respond in kind. A worker at the Eagle Works put it this way in 1921: "After all, the first demand of labor is not for bigger wages . . . The men want their bosses to recognize that they are men with all the pride, the self-respect and the right to happiness of every other human being. A few years ago the company had missed out on the human touch. Since we have had the Representation Plan, however, the circuits are connected up."

The agreement

By the spring of 1918, with the war at its height, the three New Jersey plants had finished their elections. Each plant held a formal meeting and adopted a joint agreement between men and management to be the basis for all future negotiations. The agreement provided for a personnel department charged with administering rules relating to hiring, firing and transfer, and also charged with counseling workers. It stipulated no discrimination because of union, church or club membership. It set forth the specific offenses for which an employee could be discharged, such as smoking in the refinery, violation of other safety rules, drunkenness, and so forth. For offenses *not* on the list, the company could not discharge men arbitrarily.

The 1918 agreement was a kind of Magna Charta for Jersey's employees, foremen and top management. Its spirit still broods over the contracts negotiated in 1946. The basic provisions appear and reappear throughout the thirty years of peace. Mr. Hicks in his book on industrial relations gives the seventeen-point program which was first worked out for the Colorado Fuel and Iron Company, and later instituted at Standard. Among the points were these:

No discrimination.
Collective bargaining via the Plan.
All grievances to be cleared through the Plan.
The company to pay prevailing wages or better.
The eight-hour day, and one day's rest in seven.
Special attention to safety measures.
Sickness, accident, death and disability benefits.
Special training for those who want to advance.
Promotion according to both ability and seniority.

In 1920 the program was enlarged to include savings plans to promote workers' security. For every dollar the worker put up, the company also made a contribution. In 1922 regular vacations with pay for all employees were introduced.

In due course Mr. Hicks laid down a further important provision: *Print the company's labor policy and distribute it to all employees*. Get it down in black and white, so every worker can always hold the company to its promised word. "You pledged yourself to pay prevailing wages but you are not paying *me* prevailing wages." The company must never be in a position to have such a charge made against it.

Another important policy introduced at an early date was to let workers know in advance of changes affecting them. If a lay-off was unavoidable, the men affected were warned ahead of time.

High wages, the highest in the industry, wide margins of security by means of the benefit and thrift plans, an open door for advancement—all began to build up an enduring loyalty.

I talked to a mechanic who said that after working in shops and mines and lumber camps all over the country, he came back to New Jersey, where he was born, "to make a career" for himself at Standard. "That's what we do here," he said. It sounded a little like the State Department.

As the years went by, turnover rates declined. The proportion of men who had been with the company, ten, fifteen, twenty years, increased.

The Plan expands

From New Jersey Mr. Hicks moved on to refineries in Baltimore, Md., in Parkersburg, W. Va., Charleston, S. C., and Baton Rouge, La. Later the Plan spread to the marketing divisions, and to the shops and field operations of various subsidiaries.

At Baton Rouge the boilermakers belonged to the AF of L and were on strike at the time. Mr. Hicks spent an evening explaining the Plan to them, after which the strike was called off and they voted unanimously to support the Plan. The president of the local was elected one of the workers' representatives.

The Negro workers at Baton Rouge were astonished and pleased to be invited to elect representatives from their own ranks. Their rights were exactly the same as those of the white workers, but they were organized into a separate section. They still are, for Baton Rouge is in the Deep South.

All through the 1920's, as Jersey Standard expanded its operations, the Plan was installed in new plants. By 1933 there were more than forty local unions, with an equal number of agreements, negotiating with management on all phases of labor relations. No serious strikes had occurred in any area of Standard's far-flung operations. Just as a strike can poison relations for a long time after it is settled, so good teamwork can keep on improving relations.

The Plan became famous. Other companies studied it; university sociologists analyzed it. At Princeton in 1931 an address was given by an official of the Telephone Company who ascribed the success of the Plan to three fundamentals:

1. Its unqualified acceptance by top management.

2. The encouragement of workers to state frankly what bothered them, with sure knowledge that there would be no reprisals, however severe their criticisms.

3. Regular, continued, well-organized joint conferences.

Reporting to the Department of Commerce in 1933, Walter Teagle, then president of Jersey Standard, summarized his experience of fifteen years with the Plan. The employee representatives, he declared, are not overawed or out-talked by officials of the company. They honestly represent the men who elect them. The primary purpose of the Plan is "not to draw up lines of battle but to provide means for peaceful settlement." Since most questions between men and management deal with local shop conditions, machinery must be available to handle them at once, before the snowball grows. In one operating unit, out of 6,000 grievances in fifteen years 4,000 were settled as the workers' representatives recommended.

Two powerful groups fought the Plan, Mr. Teagle observed: bosses of the old school who were afraid of giving workers any power, and AF of L leaders who said that company unions were a makeshift substitute for real unions. During the 1920's employee representation had been adopted by many companies, chiefly in the new mass production industries. These vast "vertical" industries were not adapted to the horizontal structure of AF of L craft unions. When the CIO came along years later it picked up many of the "company unions." The CIO was specifically organized for vertical industries.

Mr. Hicks spent fifteen years developing the Plan at Jersey Standard and then retired in 1933. He had worked his way up to leadership in the industrial relations field after being farm-hand, carpenter, waterfront laborer, storekeeper, foundry worker, schoolteacher, clerk in a state legislature, and finally head of railroad YMCA work. This last role once took him to Russia to sell the idea to a grand duke. He was a great pioneer and, interestingly enough, a contemporary of that other pioneer, Frederick W. Taylor. Taylor, the father of scientific management, dealt primarily in *materials*. Hicks dealt in *men,* and for the long swing his work, I think, will prove to be the more important. His book, *My Life in Industrial Relations,* should be better known.

The depression

The Roosevelt Administration changed the official status of the Employees' Representation Plan at Standard without changing its central core. The depression at its lowest point reduced Jersey Standard's payroll by about a tenth. The Baton Rouge refinery was hit the worst. Hours were cut to thirty-two a week to help "share the work." Later, as business picked up, hours were increased to thirty-six and then to forty.

Other industries meanwhile cut payrolls, not by a tenth, but 30, 40, 50 per cent. Why did the oil business weather the depression better than most? One big reason was because demand held up. People stopped buying cars but they did not stop driving them. So far as Jersey Standard was concerned, that company leaned over backward to keep on its men. (Proof is found in the attitude of the workers in a survey conducted some years later by Elmo Roper. A rousing majority in both Bayway and Baton Rouge refineries said the company "does all it can to keep workers on the job through times of slow business." Only a very small minority thought that Standard hired and fired too freely when business conditions changed.)

The NRA Act of 1933 gave American workers the right to organize and bargain collectively "through representatives of their own choosing." The representatives at Jersey Standard felt themselves freely elected, and the NRA had little or no effect on labor-management relations there.

The Wagner Act

But the Wagner Act of 1935 was something else again. In administering the Act, the National Labor Relations Board held that practically all employee representation plans were company unions, and "tainted at the source." Jersey Standard's legal counsel at that time, however, advised that the Wagner Act was unconstitutional, and would be thrown out by the Supreme Court. The learned brethren had forgotten the famous citation from Mr. Dooley[6] to the effect that the Supreme Court follows the election returns. In 1937 the Court approved the Wagner Act, and held that company unions were not bona fide agencies for collective bargaining.

[6]Finley Peter Dunne, a commentator for the *Chicago Journal* around the turn of the century, created Mr. Dooley as a mouthpiece for his sharp political and social satire. His collected comments still make good reading today.

DRILLER

GREASE PLANT
WORKMAN

STILL OPERATOR

That was the end everywhere of company unions, and of employee representation plans as such. There are said to be none in the United States today. The management of Jersey Standard announced that the Plan could not continue. The men were bewildered and distressed. It was like being expelled from school without a reason. What was the next step? Either get along with no organization at all, or form a new one which would be legal under the Wagner Act. In other oil companies, and other industries, company unions joined the CIO, as noted before, but not at Jersey Standard.[7]

Labor lawyers were called in by the workers to help them set up new unions independent enough to pass the test. This step was taken throughout the company, wherever a Jersey Standard Plan had been in operation. New constitutions, by-laws, contracts with the company were drafted, and collective bargaining resumed. Anyone who hinted to a labor official that his new union was "company dominated" would have done well to wear a catcher's mask.

CIO vs. Independents

The story now gets pretty complicated, but I will try to show the highlights. In 1942 the Oil Workers International Union, CIO, turned its attention to the refineries of Standard in New Jersey and organized some of the men. A complaint was filed with the Regional Labor Relations Board, charging that the independent unions at Bayonne and Bayway were not in fact independent. The Board ordered them dissolved. The

[7] In talking to the men, I found considerable reluctance to "join a civil war," as they phrased it. The mighty rows between the CIO and the AF of L did nothing to wean them from their local unions.

25

independents appealed to the Circuit Court, but the Court upheld the Board, and the unions stood dissolved.

Whereupon the workers proceeded to form new independent unions—the *third* set since the Wagner Act. New officers were elected, new constitutions drawn up, and the Labor Board invited to hold an election to see if the rank and file wanted these new unions or the CIO. By a vote of more than four to one at both refineries, the Independents won.

The Labor Board then certified them as the duly constituted bargaining agencies for workers at Jersey Standard. New contracts were drawn up with the company, under which men and management are operating today. In them you can still trace the basic principles laid down by Mr. Hicks. Unions come and unions go but the hardy ideas in the original seventeen-point program survive.

Dr. J. Raymond Walsh, a Harvard economics teacher who subsequently became director of the CIO Research Bureau, made a careful study of the Independents at Jersey Standard ten years or so ago. After attending many meetings and reading hundreds of pages of minutes, he concluded that they were *not* company dominated. While his preference was for international unions rather than local independents, he said it was difficult for an international to enter the field if the men were satisfied with local conditions and their local union.

This makes sense. The primary thing in labor relations is not organization machinery but human happiness and satisfaction. One should look first at the faces of the men.

The war

Jersey Standard was generous to its servicemen. All employees with more than a year's service got full pay for the

26

first two months in the Army and Navy; thereafter, if they had dependents, the company helped make up the difference between civilian and service pay with an amount not exceeding half of regular company pay. Their jobs were held for them. The Training-Within-Industry programs of the War Manpower Commission were introduced throughout the company. Labor-management committees were formed in all refineries, but it was discovered that most of the functions, as outlined by the War Production Board—except car pooling—were already being handled by the regular machinery. Long before the war, joint committees had been working on safety campaigns, the elimination of waste, salvaging materials, and encouraging suggestions for company improvements from workers. The last was known as the "Coin-Your-Ideas" program.

Meanwhile, experts at Bayway and Baton Rouge perfected the process for producing 100 octane gasoline in volume by a new catalytic cracking operation. They like to think in Jersey Standard that they saved Britain by getting the gas to the Spitfires when it was touch and go. It is quite possible they are right.

We are beginning, I think, to get some light on our original queries about the absence of strikes, the high percentage of returning servicemen, the low turnover rates. For a generation managers and men have operated in an atmosphere of mutual tolerance and respect.

Let us go into the plants and look at the situation today.

PART TWO

The Inventory Today

JERSEY STANDARD in the spring of 1946 employed about 37,000 people eligible for union membership. Altogether there were sixty-six unions. Each union was a legitimate agency for collective bargaining. Either the National Labor Relations Board had certified it as such after an election, or no group of workers had challenged the right of the union so to act. Contracts covered wages, hours and working conditions. Most of them were renewed each year. Better than 90 per cent of these eligibles were paying union dues. Here is the line-up:

	ELIGIBLES
55 Independent unions	35,884
6 CIO locals	353
4 AF of L locals	455
1 Railroad Brotherhood local	30
Total eligibles	36,722

The CIO locals were operating in small refineries in Montana, in a coke plant in West Virginia, in marine work at Bayonne, in a bulk plant in Detroit. The AF of L locals included the electricians at the Baton Rouge refinery, the machinists and electricians at the Baytown, Texas, plant of the Humble Oil & Refining Company, and operating engineers at New Castle, Wyoming. The railway brothers were switching tank cars at Baytown.

Among the Independents we find unions composed of wage workers only, salaried workers only, wage and salaried workers combined, maritime unions, laboratory unions, professional men's unions.

Thus Jersey Standard presents a kind of labor union zoo, with all the major animals on view. But the biggest animals are of one species—the Independents. In some cases men hold cards in *both* an Independent and a local of the AF of L or CIO.

In the whole United States today there are about fifteen and a half million organized workers. Seven million are said to be in the AF of L, nearly six and a half million in the CIO, approximately two million in the Independents, including the Railroad Brotherhoods, the Telephone Workers and such unions as those of Jersey Standard.

Hours and wages

When the United States entered World War II the regular work week at Jersey Standard refineries was forty hours. Operations were continuous, twenty-four hours a day, seven days a week; and workers, except in the office and mechanical departments, were divided into three shifts. The war pushed the work week up to forty-eight hours with time-and-a-half over forty. After V-J Day most operations went back to forty hours. This would have reduced take-home pay about 23 per cent (from 52 units to 40). But a 15 per cent increase in hourly rates went into effect in September 1945. Later, after the government set a kind of national pattern for an 18 per cent increase, an additional 3 per cent rise was negotiated by the Jersey Standard unions.

Did the government follow them, or did they follow the

government? Did Jersey Standard's 15 per cent in September stimulate the strike of 60,000 CIO oil workers later in the fall, or did the strike enable the workers at Standard to get another 3 per cent? These are difficult questions. Some workers to whom I talked felt that they were the indirect beneficiaries of the strike, and were a little uneasy about it. Most, however, asserted that they had started it all by the 15 per cent boost at V-J Day, and that the oil workers of the country owed *them* a vote of thanks.

The New York Times prepared a chart on June 9, 1946, with these figures on it:

	AVERAGE HOURLY EARNINGS	INCREASES SINCE V-J DAY	
		AMT. PER HOUR	PER CENT
Oil industry	$1.42	$.22	18.3
Automobiles	1.30	.18	16.1
Railroads	1.28	.185	16.9
Steel	1.245	.185	17.5
Electrical industry	1.195	.185	18.3
Soft coal	1.185	.185	17.3

Oil is out in front on all counts, though in percentage increase it runs a dead heat with the electrical industry. The average wage earner at the New Jersey plants of Standard was taking home $262 a month in 1945, and $250 in 1946. The decline in war overtime pay has hurt his pay envelope, but not greatly. In 1939, he drew an average of $153 a month.

Stillmen are among the highest paid wage earners. Right now they make $1.85 an hour at the Bayway refinery, $1.845 at the Baton Rouge refinery—which gives them about $3,800 a year. A mechanic's helper gets $1.32 an hour at Bayway;

$1.245 at Baton Rouge. The lowest rate I could find was for colored janitress beginners, seventy-one cents an hour at Baton Rouge. Compare this with seventeen cents an hour for firemen on the old crude oil stills!

Technology and jobs

In the days of World War I, a battery of twenty pressure stills could produce 2,760 gallons of mediocre gasoline in an hour. The Fluid catalytic cracking unit of 1941 produced 16,000 gallons of super-duper gasoline in an hour. About the same number of operators were required for each process.

Has this great increase in efficiency led to technological unemployment? The answer seems to be no. The men displaced by better machines and processes have been transferred to other parts of the plant. The mounting demand for oil products has kept them all at work.

Veterans

At Baton Rouge I talked at some length with three war veterans, one of them a glider pilot whose dramatic story of a rescue in New Guinea made the *Reader's Digest*. All of them were pleased with their seniority treatment. They were not yet sure that returning veterans could all make the grade.

"What happens," I asked, "if you can't make the grade?"

"Then we go to school. The company has special training courses to prepare us for new jobs."

"Is it always a better job than you left?"

"Always. We get the seniority we would have earned if we'd never gone into the service. You don't always get what you had your heart on, but you always get upgraded."

WORKER ON
'CAT CRACKER'

BOATSWAIN

TANK CAR LOADER

"What happens to the men who are pushed out to make room for the veterans?"

"Well, they get transferred to something about as good. Matter of fact, sometimes a man is transferred to something he likes better. We've heard no gripes. The men seem to think we deserve it."

This seniority procedure was negotiated by the unions and the company in March 1944. Two years later, the Supreme Court approved substantially the same thing as the right of veterans the nation over. The only criticism I heard came from the electricians in one of the refineries. "Veterans are being upgraded too high in some cases. They may deserve it, but they just haven't the know-how in a skilled craft. Somebody's going to get in an accident."

The look of a refinery

Jersey Standard workers are doing everything, from drilling a mile into the earth to running an electronic microscope. The big battalions, however, are in the refineries, helping the machines turn out gasoline and other products. The workers do not make the gasoline, the machines do that; but the workers keep the machines in order, read the meters, open and shut valves to control the never-ending stream of oil.

From a distance, a refinery is a distinctive piece of engineering. Against the sky one sees a delicate tracery of pipes and towers. Slim tall cylinders of steel, some bare, some completely clothed in what look like fire escapes, with the "cat cracker" looming above everything. The tank farm stands in the refinery's suburbs, with tanks in their flashing aluminum paint like giant silver mushrooms, and an endless maze of pipes, now on the surface, now on a kind of elevated railroad, now diving underground, now shooting 200 feet into the air. Where are they going? Who has the brain to sort them out?

The control rooms remind one of the power house at Boulder Dam, or the conning tower of a battleship. Sea or river is never far away, with the high curving bows of docked tankers. Over everything hangs a faint, pervasive smell of oil.

One night I drove across the Mississippi River bridge, and looked back through the mist at the Baton Rouge refinery. Against a gala background of multi-colored lights, winking and glowing at the water's edge and up to the sky, rose the orange flares from the vent pipes. Dante's Inferno superimposed upon a World's Fair.

Men under the towers

I visited Bayonne and Bayway as well as Baton Rouge. I talked to union officers, foremen, higher-ups, personnel people, engineers, scientists. My outstanding impression was the lack of human tension. These men seemed to get along with toleration if not positive liking. I failed to detect the scent of grudges, or of people pushing other people around. As I walked to lunch at the cafeteria with superintendents, it was "Hullo Bill, Hullo Tom, Hullo Sid," all along the line, with Bill in overalls and Sid sporting a Phi Beta Kappa key.

First and last, I have been in a good many large industrial plants. I can remember none with a more friendly atmosphere. I watched managers and superintendents for a hint of paternalism or phoney good fellowship, and found none. They seemed to accept their men the way a football coach accepts his team: "Maybe they aren't quite as smart as I am but they do the playing; where would I be without them?"

It must take many patient years to build an atmosphere

like this. A big strike wrecks team play for a long time. You can't call your team mates "communist," "agitator," "tool of Wall Street," "liar," "red," "exploiter"—and then expect to kiss and make up in a few minutes. Trigger-fingered executives and strike leaders forget they have to live with one another when the shooting is over. There has been no shooting at Jersey Standard now for a long, long time.

"Sure we get mad at each other," said a plant manager, pointing at the president of the Independent union across the table. "I get mad as hell. Then Jack here gets mad as hell. But we're careful not to get mad at the same time."

I asked a union official in New Jersey if the new contract would not be a difficult thing to negotiate. He said it would be, long and tough.

"Suppose you can't agree, and the whole machinery breaks down?"

He thought a moment and then he said, "It never has broken down, but if it did, I think we'd carry on almost as smoothly without it. You see, we trust each other."

Are the Independents independent?

I asked AF of L electrical workers at one of the refineries if they thought the Independent union was dominated by the company. They said no, but it was not so independent as their AF of L local. "We can get in the old bus and blow out of here any time we don't like the buttons on the super's vest, and get another good job anywhere in the country. The whole local could get up and go."

"Isn't that in part because you are members of a very skilled craft?" I asked.

They agreed that it was so. Also they said they were not

thinking of going immediately. They liked their homes with the paid-up mortgage; they liked the company benefits, and they belonged to the fine medical cooperative which the workers ran. They were, in fact, standing pat.

I spoke to the officials of two small independent unions of pilots and engineers operating vessels on the Mississippi. It was in June 1946, and news of an approaching maritime strike was filling all the headlines.

"Won't those men better your condition if they win their strike?" I inquired.

My conferees became pretty annoyed at this. "No," they said, "those birds are striking to get conditions as good as we have right now!"

I asked a foreman if he often had to discharge men in the line of duty. He looked mulish. "It takes an Act of Congress to fire a man around here," he said.

At Baton Rouge, I found the Independent union vigorously opposing the "open shop" bill in the state legislature.

"You have an open shop here!" I said.

"Yes, we have, but the bill is aimed at organized labor, and we're the best organized labor in this state!"

Joint conference

What do management and men discuss at one of their joint conferences? I have before me the minutes of a conference at one of the refineries in July 1945.

Twenty-one delegates from the Independent union are present and nineteen managers, including the top echelon. There are no staff officials from New York; matters coming up will be decided by line officers at the plant. The staff people advise; the line acts.

One of the managers is elected chairman of the meeting. All the afternoon discussion is lively over such questions as these:

What is to be our joint policy when the war ends, and take-home pay declines sharply?

What is the War Labor Board doing about the 5 per cent differential for shift salary employees?

Should we jointly ask the War Labor Board to liberalize Executive Order 9240, covering holiday overtime?

Should the five-year guarantee provision in the Thrift Plan be modified?

Should the distribution of overtime among department employees be changed?

Should we give trucks an arrival deadline to reduce the overtime of those who load them?

How about the condition of washrooms and lockers in the Paraflow Plant?

How soon after a man falls ill should sickness benefits be paid?

The union at Bayway is called the Independent Petroleum Workers of New Jersey. It has an executive board of forty members, and many active committees reporting to the board. From September 1, 1944 to June 1, 1946, the IPW joined in 416 meetings with management. The chief topics were grievances, job rates, seniority. Union officials devoted 5,102 man-hours to these meetings; management 3,537.

At the present time the union is demanding another wage increase, four weeks' vacation after twenty years of service, representation on company benefit plans, increases in overtime pay for shift work, and so on. Altogether, twenty union demands are up for negotiation.

It is not surprising that a manager at Bayway said to me a little sadly: "We have so many joint conferences around here, it's a wonder we have any time left to get out oil."

"What are you going to do about it?" I asked.

"Well," he said, "I guess we'll have to let one top executive at the plant do nothing but labor relations, while another gets out the oil. It's no longer a one-man job."

This illustrates Jersey Standard's attitude as well as anything I know. *Men are just as important as production.*

How do workers feel?

As I went about the refineries, talking to men and management, three impressions of how workers feel at Jersey Standard began to form in my mind. Again and again, this three-point pattern was visible.

1. We like our work here. We don't know where we could go to find a better company to work for.

2. We like our union organization. It deals with our own local problems and we like that. It gives us a feeling of solidarity and independence. Nobody is pushing us around.

3. Top management is always fair. Foremen are pretty good on the whole, but they need to be checked up now and then on the carrying out of company policy. One worker said to me: "If they dealt with foremen as well as they deal with us, we'd have quite a company." (Foremen, of course, are a growing problem in industrial relations everywhere today.)

Criticisms

I found no evidence of any deep-seated grievances against management. The bitter proclamations which accompanied the strikes at Bayonne in 1916 have vanished. One finds a certain amount of criticism of local conditions. For instance, workers in the refineries at Bayonne and Bayway think that more vacations should come in the summer.

Union officials think that they should have more to say about company benefit plans.

The awards for workers' suggestions, in the "Coin-Your-Ideas" program, do not result in very much coin. This burns up some of the amateur Edisons, and is a just criticism, I think.

Some workers say that the union ought to be jointly responsible with management for job analysis studies, which form the basis for wage rates.

A deeper resentment appears in the South. At Baton Rouge I found the Negro workers greatly distressed because of the obstacles to advancement. They belong to the same union as the white workers, with the same company contract, but they are organized in a Negro section, and most of their members fill the lower-paid jobs. Many, they feel, are qualified by education and character to hold better jobs. It is sad to see so many good men forced to work below their abilities.

If I might venture a criticism of the union officials it is that they seem to be too exclusively concerned with local shop problems. They should have more contact with other plants, and generally raise their sights a bit in this year two of the atomic age.

These are my impressions of how workers feel at the refineries, but we do not have to leave it at that. They are confirmed by three surveys of employee opinion made by Elmo Roper, the first at Baton Rouge in 1945, the second and third at Bayway in 1946.

Mr. Roper has a good story about selling the idea of the poll to one of the unions. The men were silent for a while, until finally an official spoke up. "I'm for it," he said. "It's a good idea and here's why. I tell the management what the workers want. They want this and they want that, and I bang the table. So Bill here (the superintendent) he says no, that's not what the workers want, they want that and they want this. And *he* bangs the table. But neither of us knows a damn thing about what the workers *really* want. I'm for Mr. Roper finding out."

The Roper poll preserves complete anonymity. This is explained to the men in advance so effectively that their answers are frank. Using the sampling method, the poll gets an accurate cross section of everyone in the plant. I am going to pick out, from the thirty-five or more questions, fifteen which struck me as especially significant. Instead of giving the percentages, I will divide the replies into three categories—"yes plus" meaning 75 per cent of the total replies or more; "yes" meaning 51 to 75 per cent; "no" meaning a negative plurality. I will also take some liberties in abbreviating Mr. Roper's carefully worded questions.

What I am trying to show is the spirit of the men, the mass reaction of workers to their jobs. Following Mr. Roper, I give separate reports for the refinery at Bayway, and for the Standard Oil Development Company, meaning the laboratory workers. Manual and clerical workers are combined in all reports. The approximate number of union workers at Baton

FOREMAN

TRAFFIC CLERK

Rouge is 8,000; at the Bayway refinery 3,300; at the Development Company 900.

REACTION OF ALL WORKERS

	BATON ROUGE REFINERY 1945	BAYWAY REFINERY 1946	DEVELOP- MENT CO. BAYWAY 1946
Standard is better than the average company	yes	yes plus	yes plus
I want to make my career at Standard	(not asked)	yes plus	yes
I like my job	yes plus	yes plus	yes plus
I like my fellow workers	yes plus	yes plus	yes plus
Top management is fair and decent	yes plus	yes plus	yes plus
It takes a real interest in my happiness	yes	yes	yes
It thinks my job is important	yes	yes	yes
It helps the workers in a depression	yes	yes plus	yes plus
It considers me a human being, not a number on the payroll	yes	yes	yes
I like my foreman	yes plus	yes	yes plus
He is not a slave driver	yes plus	yes plus	yes plus
He welcomes my suggestions	yes	yes	yes
He shows no favoritism	no	yes	yes
My favorite company policy is	sick benefits	sick benefits	promotion system
A big company is better to work for than a small one	yes	yes	yes

The mass reaction is clear enough. Workers at Jersey Standard like their jobs, their fellow workers, the top management. They are afraid the foreman shows some favoritism, but he is not a slave driver and he welcomes suggestions. The two

41

things the workers like best are the company benefit programs and the opportunity to advance.

Breaking the total refinery figures down by groups at Baton Rouge, Mr. Roper notes that women workers, Negroes and technicians are not as well satisfied as the others. The strongest complaint in all three surveys was favoritism by foremen, but only in Baton Rouge did a plurality of the workers believe this.

Mr. Roper found, as I found, resentment by Negroes of the narrow opportunities for bettering their position. Technical workers, both North and South, were also somewhat worried about advancement. There was some criticism of the seniority rule in promotion, of the rule against smoking, of cafeterias and washrooms, of some provisions in the Thrift Plan, of means of getting from place to place inside the huge plant areas.

In concluding his report, Mr. Roper reminds us of the four great human desires which come out strongly in *all* surveys of public opinion, Jersey Standard being no exception. They are:

1. Economic security
2. A chance to better oneself
3. To be treated like a person
4. To feel one's job is important to the community

By and large, these cardinal desires seem to be reasonably well satisfied at Baton Rouge and Bayway. That was the way I felt about it as a lone observer; that is the way the Roper survey comes out. It is too bad we do not have a string of parallel surveys of many big corporations by which to determine the relative rating of Jersey Standard. I suspect it would be high.

PART THREE

Broader Aspects

STRIKES have ceased; workers are pretty well satisfied, conditions are relatively good at Jersey Standard. The plans which Mr. Hicks introduced, amid skepticism by men and management after the bloody business at the Bayonne refinery, have proved their worth. What have students of labor-management problems to learn from this thirty-year experiment? Would it work as well in other industries?

Riding a trend

The careful student cannot fail to note that Jersey Standard's problem has been simplified because of two historical trends.

The first is *expansion*. The American people have been going motorcar crazy ever since Ford introduced Model T. There is no need to fortify this statement with figures. Five, ten, twenty, thirty million cars on the road demand an ocean of gasoline, a constantly expanding ocean! The oil business accordingly has been an automatically expanding business, with practically no problem of sales resistance. Even in the depression, when people stopped buying new cars, they kept on buying gasoline.

The second trend is *continuity*. The technology of oil pro-

43

duction demands, for low-cost performance, continuous year-round operation without large seasonal swings and shutdowns. People buy gas and oil in steady volume the year round too. The production of motorcars has been handicapped by the annual model fashion cycle, resulting in seasonal spurts. This is hard on management; harder on men. By contrast the production of oil has been so steady that most workers at Standard already enjoy substantially an "annual wage." When gasoline sales ease off a little with cold weather in the fall, the demand for fuel oil helps to fill the gap.

Continuous employment is a great builder of worker morale. The employee can plan his future, buy a house, raise a family, plant a garden, become a responsible citizen in his community. At Baton Rouge you can see the workers' houses, many of them set in gardens for "twilight farming," scattered over a radius of fifty miles from the refinery. The first lesson for the student lies right here. The better you can balance your operating load, the better your labor relations.

If Mr. Hicks had worked an equal time with coal, or steel, or textiles, where expansion has been spotty, and the seasonal factor great, he would have found harder going, I think. Automatic expansion, furthermore, encourages a liberal wage policy. Direct labor costs in relation to total costs are relatively low. Wages tend to be high in any industry where the ratio of labor cost to total cost is low, where horsepower per worker is high, where profits are ample.

Other large oil companies, however, have had the same long swing advantages. Many of them have had more labor troubles than Standard, and in 1945, as we have seen, they shut up shop in a nation-wide strike.

44

Five causes

There seem to be five major reasons for Jersey Standard's long period without serious strikes, in addition to the outside assets of expansion and continuity. Let us list them first and then go back and discuss some of them in more detail. They overlap in part but for purposes of analysis we will separate them:

1. The persistent, firm realization by top management that workers are human beings and not commodities.

2. The continuous stressing of workers' *security* in the form of benefit plans. Public opinion polls show that this policy is right on the trend curve. Employment and security are tied together. The demand for them is primary and massive all over the civilized world.

3. The policy of paying prevailing wages or better, thus helping security by a relatively high wage scale.

4. The recognition by the company that a large corporation in this day and age has at least four publics to serve: workers, consumers, stockholders, and the general public as represented by the government. Relations must run smoothly with each of these groups, or the corporation will find itself in deep water.

5. The recognition by management of the necessity of teamwork in modern industry.

Workers are people

There is considerable difference between the paternal attitude and the fraternal attitude. So far as I could judge, managers at Jersey Standard regard their workers as people as good as themselves (except for some race prejudice in the South). Managers did not look down their noses at the Grievance Committee, or whatever the workers' group might be. They looked horizontally across the table.

This democratic attitude extends to the ranks of management itself. A high executive once asked Mr. Hicks if he, the executive, had the right man for the head of his labor relations department.

"Does he look you in the eye from time to time and tell you you're wrong?"

"No."

"Better get one who will."

My mind keeps coming back to the worker in New Jersey who told me that men and management would get along almost as smoothly if there were no collective bargaining machinery. The two groups trusted each other, and that was the main thing. I doubt if the worker fully realized how important bargaining machinery becomes when an organization grows as large as Jersey Standard—but he had grasped something fundamental.

At this point, however, we discover a theoretically vulnerable spot. Suppose a new management comes in with a different policy—the E. H. Harriman policy for instance: "I don't want anything in this railroad I can't control." What happens to the workers then? The AF of L electricians at Baton Rouge can get into the old bus and drive to the next local, but the Independents have no cash reserves in their treasuries, and no outside organizations to back them up. I asked a group of workers: "What do you do if this management is replaced by the old-fashioned kind?" Their faces registered consternation.

46

"They wouldn't do that to us."

Certainly the present management would not, but suppose somebody else does? There seem to be two answers. The men now are well organized and disciplined at the plant level. They could merge their power into a single union embracing all of Jersey Standard's operations—something like the Telephone Workers' organization. Instead of fifty-five bargaining groups there would be one. This would be a tough outfit to face a tough management. Or they could join an outside international union as so many other independents have done.

This difficulty, however, is very remote. The present management seems to like its job, and it has been in power for a long time. Stockholders are not complaining. As younger men replace older ones, they tend to conform; they would hardly be foolish enough to throw overboard the profitable methods of thirty years.

Suppose, in some future Labor Relations Board election, all the Independents voted to join the AF of L, or the CIO, or some new international union? Suppose labor policies continue as they have for thirty years—not necessarily the forms but the spirit? What would happen?

My guess is that not a great deal would happen. The most important thing would be largely unaffected—the human relationship between management and men. The international union would have to adjust to that reality.

Speaking of reality, consider the average American manager. He thinks of himself as a realist. He is the chap who meets payrolls while others dream. Benjamin M. Selekman in his article, *Wanted: Mature Managers*,[8] drives a bulldozer through this cozy notion. "Instead of accepting shop reality as

[8] *Harvard Business Review*, Winter 1946.

an organic social whole of many material and non-material factors in inter-relation, he partializes it into considerations of money, materials and machines that are 'real' even when they are difficult—and of men who are cussed or 'unreasonable' when *they* are difficult." Thus the average manager becomes thoroughly unrealistic on the level of action.

No thing around the shop is more real than the people who work in it. Managers who think money, materials and machines are the only realities leave out the most important characteristic of successful management—the understanding of men. Managers of Jersey Standard do not leave this characteristic out.

Security

A union man said to me: "We used to think money was the most important thing in negotiating; now we know it isn't. A steady job and security are more important." The Roper survey backs him up. After years of testing public opinion Mr. Roper concludes, in an article in the *Survey Graphic*: "The thing most demanded for our country by most people, of all economic levels, and in all walks of life, is continuity of employment."

This emphatic mass demand has been recognized at Jersey Standard. The company has been acting upon it for many years. The Plan as originally conceived by Mr. Hicks included these provisions:

1. Sickness disability benefits—after one year's service with the company.

2. Accident disability payments.

3. Medical supervision by a competent staff.

DISTRICT CHIEF CLERK

PRODUCT METER CHECKER

4. Death benefits at company expense, and group life insurance at low cost.

5. Annuities for life at normal retirement age, after twenty years of service.

6. Helping the employee to buy company stock, by adding fifty cents to each dollar he invested.

7. Special training courses for ambitious employees.

This was a remarkable program a generation ago. All the items are still on the books except the stock ownership plan. The SEC regulations make it difficult to carry this out, so the Jersey Standard stock acquisition plan has been changed to a "thrift plan," whereby the company helps employees to save.

The educational program has been expanded to embrace not only training for the job but general education. The ambitious program for veterans has already been mentioned. Recreation programs have been expanded. Time off with pay is now allowed when workers are on jury duty, drilling with the National Guard, or performing other civic obligations. There is an important idea here: the worker wins recognition not only as a member of the company, *but as a member of the community*.

"Coin-Your-Ideas" is another addition to the original Hicks' program. It resembles the famous suggestion-box campaign carried on by labor-management committees during the war. Standard had it long before the war, as noted earlier. In 1945, 4,972 suggestions for improvements were received from employees, of which 2,219 were accepted, most with a cash payment. The awards are pretty low relative to the estimated savings, running about 3 per cent of savings in 1945. They should be substantially raised, for the idea is fundamentally sound. It helps to give the workers some understanding of management's problems. They become jointly responsible for making improvements.

Perhaps the most interesting benefit plan of all is run by the workers themselves. At Baton Rouge the white employees in 1923 organized a cooperative medical association, with their own doctors, nurses, clinic, and hospital insurance. There are now a dozen doctors, and the plan is very popular. A pipefitter with three children told me that his wife figured they had saved at least $5,000 in medical outlays in the fifteen years they had been members of "Stanocola." The Negro workers are hoping to start an association something like it.

I hope they do. It helps workers understand the function of management when they manage things themselves. Peter F. Drucker remarked in his recent book on corporations: "It is doubtful whether management is not today doing far too much for the worker, instead of letting him do it for himself."

The benefit plans at Jersey Standard are considered not paternalism but good business, as Mr. Hicks pointed out many years ago. Part of the accident insurance program is a safety-first campaign. In Baton Rouge, the boilermakers' department went from August 17, 1938 to April 25, 1945, a total of 3,316,-533 man-hours, without a disabling accident! This performance is probably a world's record.

Four publics

In 1922 the labor policy of Jersey Standard was printed in a small gray pamphlet and distributed to all employees. Its foreword explains that the policy is based on the fundamental idea of a square deal for all concerned—the employees, the management, the stockholders and the general public. In later editions management was cut out, and *consumers* of the company's products substituted. Management is more properly the central power plant which shapes the policies to satisfy the other publics.

In the good old days, a manager was judged by his ability to keep costs down—especially wages, which used to be the major element in cost—and by the size of his profit. His chief public was the stockholder. But often he himself was the chief stockholder, or proprietor of the business. The structure of a large modern corporation in mass production is very different. Management is frequently divorced from ownership, as Berle and Means demonstrated.[9] Wages are a far smaller element of total cost. The stock may be widely held, much of it by employees of the company. The consumer must be constantly attended to—unless one has an airtight monopoly—or he will jump to a competitor. The government affects the company at many points through its tax policies, conservation laws, anti-trust legislation. Workers demand security and other rights.

So managers today have a four-ring circus to operate. Jersey Standard has kept up with the times, and recognized the structure and the obligations of the modern corporation. It is in part a money-making machine, but in greater part it is an economic agent of the community, responsible to the community. The "robber barons" of the '90's did not see things quite this way. But they are all dead. A recent editorial in THE LAMP states the company's philosophy:

> Essentials of leadership are awareness of the deep aspirations of people, and ability to provide constructive suggestions as to

[9]*The Modern Corporation and Private Property* by Adolph A. Berle, Jr., and Gardiner C. Means. (Macmillan, 1933.)

how these aspirations may be realized. If today's managers of private enterprise are to justify their positions, they must conceive their duties in broader terms than simply the production of goods. They must have a sense of public responsibility, and must assume active roles.

Philosophy of teamwork

The fourth policy of Jersey Standard which has contributed to the thirty years of peace is the idea that a factory, or an industry, should be an example of teamwork, not a struggle for power between "capital" and "labor." This idea, familiar enough in Labor Day orations, has revolutionary implications when it is actually applied to labor-management relations. We see the implication developed in the psychological research studies at Western Electric, in the work of Elton Mayo of Harvard, in the Training-Within-Industry programs, in industrial relations work at Princeton, Yale, M. I. T. and other universities.

As Elton Mayo has pointed out, *homo sapiens* is not equipped by nature to work in a factory—certainly not in the kind of factories that were developed in the nineteenth century. He is equipped by nature to roam the forests in search of game, or till the fields on his own time with no hard and fast distinction between work and play. There are no time clocks in the biological history of man.

The machine, however, is a prodigious saver of man-hours per ton produced. *Homo sapiens* perhaps has had no choice but to follow the technological road. He is now too far along it to turn back. To retreat to the handicraft age would cost most of the population of America. And the atomic age has begun. But *homo sapiens* has not been happy in his factories.

52

They have galled him, frustrated him, and often completely broken him.

Three stages in labor relations

One large field for readjustment is certainly the relations between a few human beings called managers, and a larger number of human beings called workers. This was Mr. Hicks' vineyard, and he cultivated it well. He describes three stages in industrial relations:

The *first* is the Big Boss era; you-do-what-you're-told-and-no-back-talk. Any concessions to labor are called philanthropy. The idea of teamwork is so much eyewash.

The *second* stage is a battle, sometimes violent, always intense. Labor has fought its way out of the autocratic era and set up a strong workers' organization. The two parties heave and struggle for mastery. In the belief that gross income is strictly limited, management fights for a bigger slice in dividends, labor fights for a bigger slice in wages. Teamwork is regarded by both sides as namby-pamby stuff. The public interest is completely disregarded.

The *third* stage comes when management and men realize that their livelihood depends on a healthy industry, and that no industry can remain healthy very long as a battlefield in a civil war. They begin to see the fundamental unity of their interests. In this country, said Mr. Hicks, it is no longer a question of "capital" dealing with "labor," but of management and labor dealing with stockholders, consumers and the public. A wage earner "has too large a stake in his employing corporation to treat it as something to fight." The function of management, in this stage, is to bring worker, owner and consumer together in a mutually beneficial relationship.

In sharp contrast to the alignment on the battlefield, the men facing each other in industry, even at the moments when they differ, belong in the larger sense to the same team. The men in conflict with the shop manager remain always the men with whom he must work to turn out goods.[10]

In the last year we have had a somber lesson in what is bound to happen if management and worker do not team up. The government, in a perfectly logical attempt to protect the public interest, will take the matter out of their hands.

Jersey Standard has by-passed the second stage, and for a generation has been exploring the possibilities of the third. Teamwork has been the order of the day ever since the employees accepted Mr. Hicks' idea. Not many workers with whom I talked in the refineries wanted to retreat to the fighting stage. They would prefer not to waste time hating people whom they now rather like.

The class struggle ideology, based on a system of absolutes, tends to prevent teamwork. To a worker who believes in the class struggle, the bosses look like a society of fiends. To a manager who believes in it, the workers, and especially their leaders, seem to be a gang of bums, loafers and foreign agitators. The class struggle may or may not have been a useful philosophical concept when formulated in Europe a century ago. It has never fitted conditions in the United States, except in a few remote company towns, and in other limited situations. Europe had a system of fixed classes in 1840; our classes have always been fluid. Lincoln once remarked: "There is no permanent class of hired laborers among us." Anne O'Hare McCormick extends the idea:

[10] Benjamin M. Selekman in the article quoted earlier.

III. BROADER ASPECTS

War, domestic or international, is no longer the answer to any problem. The idea that society is divided into separate classes, like the idea that the world is composed of separate nations, has to give way to modern realities. Every civil war is now a world war, and every world war is now a civil war. And in these wars there are no winners. Force has become a boomerang, wherefore man has no recourse save the use of reason.

The class struggle is an old-fashioned concept, incompatible with the growing interdependence of the power age. The recent threat of a railroad strike brought home to the whole country, from President Truman down, how helpless every man jack of us would be if food and fuel should cease to move over the transportation network. Big cities would be starved out in a few days. A power strike would be worse; a telephone strike almost as bad. A refinery strike would ground every airplane, stop every truck and motorcar in a short time.

"I am convinced," says Professor E. W. Bakke of Yale, "that two such giants as organized labor and organized management cannot thresh around in a struggle for dominance within the delicate mechanisms of the American economy . . . without bringing the whole structure down upon the heads of all of us. If they do that, the public demand for regimentation of both in order to avoid chaos will be irresistible. Such a demand will threaten the survival of free unions and free management. . . ."

Whether we like it or not, the machine age has made us our brothers' keepers. At the same time the machine promises abundance for all if we respect the technological imperatives, and play according to the rules. The first rule is to keep the machine turning over—and that demands cooperation among those who run it.

Jersey Standard has found a valuable formula for cooperation. There is plenty of meat in the record for students of labor relations. The late Sidney Hillman found a somewhat different formula. After years of battling in stage two, he led the Amalgamated Clothing Workers Union into stage three, by a policy of actively cooperating with employers to keep the industry healthy. At times the union even went so far as to loan large sums to employers from the union treasury. There has been no large strike in the men's clothing industry in thirty years.

Mr. Hillman played the game according to the rules of modern technology and the power age. So does Jersey Standard. Is the Amalgamated formula better or worse than Standard's? I am convinced, from firsthand study, that both formulas keep men reasonably satisfied, prevent big strikes, meet the pragmatic test. It is perhaps better to have men rather than management initiate the process, but we should be grateful for the result either way.

Some labor experts think it might be possible to combine the best features of each. Dr. William M. Leiserson, for instance, has suggested in the *Encyclopedia of the Social Sciences* that trade union methods of bargaining on a national scale, with the aid of trained experts chosen by the workers, might be added to employee representation plans. At the same time the regular trade unions might well adopt shop committee methods for handling local problems peculiar to each plant. Thus one would have the benefit of both decentralization and centralization.

*   *   *

Beatrice Webb, the great British sociologist, became interested in the labor movement while studying corporation reports as a young research worker in London. She kept finding statements which read like this: "Water plentiful and labor docile." This philosophy held the stage for a hundred years in Europe, and for altogether too long a period in America. People in the shops and offices of the power age are not commodities, and do not propose to be treated as such. Jersey Standard began agreeing with them in 1918. It thus grasped a revolutionary principle which runs deeper than unions, deeper than the class struggle, deep down into the fundamental nature of man himself.